SAS COVERT RURAL-REMOTE AREA SURVEILLANCE

TACTICS, TECHNIQUES, AND PROCEDURES

AUSTRALIAN SASR COUNTER TERROR MANUAL

VARANGIAN PRESS

ISBN:10-1983404705
ISBN-13:978-1983404702

DISCLAIMER

This book is intended for information purposes only. The information contained in this book is true and complete to the best of our knowledge. The author and publisher disclaim any liability in connection with the use of this information.

INFATUO MODO DISCIT AB EXPERIENTIA

"A fool learns only from experience"

CONTENTS

BRIEF HISTORY OF THE ASASR

The SASR can trace its beginnings back to the Australian Z Special Unit and Independent Commando Companies that fought during the Second World War. On 25 July 1957, the 1st Special Air Service Company, Royal Australian Infantry, was raised at Campbell Barracks, Swanbourne, in Western Australia; largely modelled on the British SAS.

"The Company consisted of a headquarters and four platoons comprising about 200 all ranks by the time it became part of The Royal Australian Regiment in 1960." At the same time it was given responsibility for commando and SF operations in the Australian Army.

On 04 September 1964, the 1st Special Air Service Company was expanded to become the Special Air Service Regiment with three sabre squadrons. Following disengagement from Vietnam in October 1971, 2 Squadron was disbanded to allow the SAS Training Squadron to be raised (later renamed the SAS Support Squadron, subsequently the Operational Support Squadron).

The SASR gained its CT remit on 23 February 1978 after a terrorist attack on the Sydney Hilton on the 13 February in the same year. In order to maintain the SASRs CT and war role capabilities, in 1982 the disbanded 2 Squadron was reformed.

CHAPTER 1

<u>INTRODUCTION</u>

Not all surveillance targets will be located in user -friendly urban areas. The target may live in a rural area or be traveling through a remote area. These types of locations provide almost ideal conditions for illegal activity such as drug or weapons transfers with very little chance of accidental discovery. If initial intelligence suggests that illegal activity will be taking place in a rural or remote area, a surveillance team should be deployed to gather further intelligence at the first available opportunity.

As rural/remote area surveillance methodology is more akin to a military operation than a standard surveillance operation, operators must learn specialized skills.

All prospective operators must be volunteers and should be informed of the inherent demands of Covert Rural/Remote Area Surveillance work. Ideally, they should also be trained and experienced mobile surveillance operators.

Prior to selection candidates should undergo a pre-selection process. Candidates should not suffer from any of the following phobias:

Agoraphobia – fear of open spaces.

Claustrophobia – fear of enclosed spaces.

Acrophobia – fear of heights.

Fear of animals, reptiles or insects.

It is recommended that CROP operators be trained over three weeks in a practical environment. At the conclusion of the training the operative will be able to:

a) Utilise fieldcraft and movement techniques by:

- Moving through open land utilising crawl techniques where appropriate; Move through a rural environment utilising natural cover;

- Stalk a subject through the rural environment utilising crawl and cover techniques;
- Change appearance to match rural environment;
- Ensure minimum disturbance to the environment whilst moving;
- Reduce to a minimum incriminating material whilst moving through rural environment;
- Identify aids to progress and obstacles in advance of selecting route; Plans and prepares efficient and covert routing through rural terrain.

b) Utilise camouflage and concealment techniques by:

- Transforming quickly from conventional dress into rural equipment; Dress appropriately for the environment;

- Utilising cover stories able to withstand scrutiny if discovered;

c) Conduct rapid deployments covertly and safely by:

- Being able to analyse quickly whether it is safe to rapidly deploy covertly from a vehicle in any location;

- Being able to rapidly deploy using a variety of appropriate methods;
  Planning and preparing for rapid deployment;
- Conducting risk assessments on rapid deployments;
  Covertly marking deployment points;
- Driving vehicles for other operators deploying;
- Secreting vehicle covertly after operative deployment and assuming back-up role.

d) Plan, prepare and occupy a Covert Rural Observation Post by:

- Undertaking comprehensive reconnaissance;

- Identifying emergency rendezvous points;
- Identifying routes into and out of CROPs;
- Conducting drop-off and pick ups;
- Being aware of contingency plans for lost communications;
- Knowing rail track safety and first aid procedures;
- Acting as support to another operative in a CROP.

e) Conduct Close Target Reconnaissance (CTR) by:

- Locating livestock and wild/domestic animals if appropriate;

- Creating CROPS where necessary;
- Planning advance compromise warnings and cover stories;
- Vehicle tracking devices covertly deployed and retrieved.

CHAPTER 2

<u>INSERTION</u>

When planning insertion for a Rural/Remote Area Surveillance Mission, There are several basic factors to be considered:

a.   Mission. The mission may require rapid deployment into the target area, which would dictate the quickest method of insertion. In most other cases, stealth would be the overriding factor and would require considerable notice to allow a stealthy approach.

b.   Target Situation. Target capabilities, experience, paranoia, security measures, location, will all affect the means selected for insertion. A paranoid enemy with known associates along the main roads leading to the target area will probably receive advance warning if a strange vehicle is seen in the area. In this case, a protracted, stealthy overland insertion by foot must be considered as the safest option.

c.   Terrain. Terrain characteristics such as type of vegetation, land formations and bodies of water must all be considered.

d.   Weather. Weather conditions will affect the insertion planning. Hot weather may preclude a day-time insertion which may in-turn affect the time able to be spent in the target area. Rain or fog may be chosen for cover.

e.   Hydrography. If the target area is located on the coast, tides and coastal weather warnings will need to be taken into account.

f.   Astronomical Conditions. Periods of twilight, sunrise, sunset, moon phases, moonrise and moonset must all be considered for insertions.

g. Distance. The distance to the target area must be considered in the selection of the means of insertion. A 20 km hike to the target area would probably preclude a foot insertion.

h. Specialised Training. Although operators receive generic training which will prepare them for foot or vehicle insertions, a waterborne or even air insertion will require specialised training.

i. Specialised equipment. Long lenses, tracking device receivers, long-range HF radios will all add weight to an already heavy load. This will affect the insertion method.

SAMPLE MISSION PLANNING MATRIX

MISSION	
	Primary Objective: ☐ To observe and record JOHN SMITH's meeting with the Sergeant At Arms of the MONGRELS Outlaw Motorcycle Gang on 06DEC2002. Secondary Objectives: ☐ Close Target Reconnaissance of the main dwelling to support future operations. ☐ Place tracking device on SMITH's Harley Davidson motorcycle.
TARGET SITUATION	SMITH is known to be paranoid and will actively and periodically check for surveillance. Additionally, SMITH has a large Alsatian dog, which has the run of the property. SMITH's cousin, JAMIE NEVILLE lives along the line of approach and telephone intercepts confirm NEVILLE has telephoned warnings of Law Enforcement Activity to SMITH in the past.
TERRAIN	The Target Area is in an arid area located in a sparsely wooded valley ringed with cliffs.
WEATHER	On insertion, weather is predicted to be hot and dry with clear sky.

HYDROGRAPHY

N/A

ASTRONOMICAL

CONDITIONS

Sunset is 1844, Sunrise 0512, Full moon, moonrise 0015, moonset 1351

DISTANCE

The Target Area is located approximately 52km from the closest town (Wallaroo).

SPECIALISED

TRAINING   N/A

REQUIRED

MISSION-CRITICAL

EQUIPMENT   Vehicle tracking device, shovel, PVC OP frame, HF radio.

CHAPTER 3

INDIVIDUAL FIELDCRAFT TECHNIQUES

Introduction

For a rural/remote area surveillance operation to be successful, the operator must be able to observe the target without he or she being observed by the target. The operator must be capable of moving to the OP point, constructing the OP, and observing and recording the target in all weather and light conditions without being detected by the target or other personnel.

The Purpose of Fieldcraft

Fieldcraft is the use of natural and artificial cover to provide a measure of protection from detection and thereby permit movement and allow the effective employment of video or photographic equipment. Fieldcraft training enables the operator, by day and night, to:

a.   Use the senses to find the target without being seen him or herself.

b.   Always make the best use of ground.

c.   Move silently with or without stores and equipment such as OP construction materials, backpacks, etc.

d.   Be alert, confident and maintain tactical awareness whatever situation may arise.

The relevance of Fieldcraft

Training in fieldcraft techniques will develop the qualities of self-reliance and mental toughness required in an operative and will impart the confidence to exploit fully the terrain to successfully complete an extended rural/remote area surveillance operation. It will also educate the operator to use nature to best advantage.

Fieldcraft is a specialised skill that takes considerable practice to master. Fieldcraft reduces the chances of being seen and therefore aids in avoiding a compromise. With the aid of fieldcraft, the operator can move as close as possible to the target thereby increasing the opportunities of capturing good imagery of the target.

Qualities of the Covert Rural/Remote Area Surveillance Operator

Fieldcraft training should make the operator feel at home in the field and help develop a sense of confidence in his/her natural qualities. Unlike covert urban surveillance, the CRSO must deal with extremes of weather, loneliness, uncomfortable and sometimes unhygienic conditions, fatigue, fear and extreme danger.

The operator may be called upon to lug a 20kg backpack for hours before moving into the OP position. Then the operator must dig the OP itself. All the while in close proximity to the target. The operator cannot cook due to the risk of compromise from light or smell, he or she must urinate into bottles and defecate into ziplock bags.

To be good at fieldcraft, the operator must refine these qualities as follows:

a. *Power of Observation.* Fieldcraft requires study of and an awareness of, the natural surroundings and the ground. The operator must be able to picture him or herself as the target would, both at close range and at a distance.

b. *Self-Discipline.* Even if the power of observation has been mastered, the operator must remain concealed while observing. This requires self-discipline and will be assisted by the following:

1. *Alertness.* Mistakes caused by lack of foresight and awareness are difficult to rectify. The operator must be alert to changes in the

immediate environment and should be encouraged to plan ahead. Alertness to preserve concealment at all times must be a habit.

2.   *Adaptability.* Concealment adequate in one place or time may be unsuitable either in another place or at a different time of day. The operator must be trained to adapt to change and adopt new or better concealment methods as conditions dictate.

These qualities will assist the operator to achieve cover and concealment from the target while providing detection and observation of the target's presence and actions.

Personal Camouflage & Concealment

To be effective in the field, the target must not detect the operative. The ability to photograph or video the target in a rural environment without being detected is a skill acquired through practice. Concealment is one of the basic tenets of covert rural/remote area surveillance. When used against hard targets or violent offenders, it can even mean the difference between life and death.

An operative uses concealment to deceive and outwit the target. To achieve effective concealment he or she must know how to adapt his or her dress to blend with the background and how to use the available vegetation and natural features of the ground.

Camouflage

Camouflage techniques are designed to deceive the target from land and the air. Effective camouflage of the individual depends primarily on the choice of background and its correct use. The term "background" is used to describe the area surrounding an object when seen from the ground or the air. It is the controlling factor in personal camouflage. The others that are worn must blend with the predominant colour of the background. Skin and light-coloured equipment are toned down for the same purpose. The operator must practise blending with the background by hiding in shadows and avoiding contrast between his silhouette and the background. To enable the operative to do this, he or she must practice the skills of camouflaging him/herself and equipment.

Camouflage is a continuing process. Camouflage on skin and clothing will need to be reapplied during strenuous activities such as OP building. The operator must always be conscious of the requirements of good camouflage and realise that it is his or her responsibility to maintain effective camouflage. Failure to do so could lead to detection by the target and compromise of the operation.

Skin

Exposed skin reflects light and contrasts with the surrounding background. Face, neck, hands and lower arms, which may be exposed below the shirt, should be toned down by painting them in a disruptive pattern, by toning them down in an even colour, or by wearing additional accessories such as a scrim scarf or nomex gloves. When using disruptive painting, patterns should cut across the nose lines, cheek bones, eye sockets, and other lines. A darker treatment of the skin will be necessary for night work. Camouflage face paint, burnt charcoal, dirt, dust and mud can all help to tone down skin colours.

Camouflage Clothing

Camouflage clothing is generally more effective than solid coloured clothing, especially when wet. The operator must select the correct camouflage pattern for the terrain in which the operation is to take place. In Australian temperate environments, the DP or "AUSCAM" uniform is the most effective. In arid or desert environments, special desert camouflage uniforms can be purchased, or the operator can simply wear tan or khaki civilian workwear such as "King Gees" which have been stained in places with coffee grounds, spray paint or grease. In a tropical or rainforest environment, "woodland" or "DPM" camouflage patterns are most useful as AUSCAM is too bright for the dark shadows found in the jungle.

The camouflage suit must look like the terrain in which it is to be worn. It must be remembered that the use of camouflage clothing and camouflaged equipment are only the basis for good concealment.

Shoes or boots

Black or brown military combat boots are good for covert rural/remote area surveillance work. They are designed for tough conditions but must be thoroughly broken in to be comfortable and to avoid foot injuries. Civilian hiking boots in a suitable "earth" colour may also be utilised and are a good choice for operators who are not used to field work. Ensure the boots are not polished or shiny. If they are, the sheen can be taken off with a nylon kitchen scourer dampened with water.

Hat

A camouflaged floppy bush hat is good for breaking up the outline of the head and for shadowing the face. Some operators will prefer an "earth" coloured baseball cap or even a camouflaged "Bandido" type bandana. Any hat has a distinctive shaped crown which can be broken up by the use of shredded hessian or a small amount of suitable vegetation.

Packs, camera vests and webbing

The solid colouring of most load bearing equipment can be modified by painting with matt finish earth coloured paints. The shape of vests and webbing equipment can be broken up by the use of hessian strips and foliage.

Cameras and other Equipment

All cameras, whether they be still or video cameras, have a distinctive shape and parts which may shine. The simplest way to distort the shape of camera equipment is to wrap it in a camouflage cloth or hessian. If the operative uses this technique, he or she must ensure that both the viewfinder and the lens are not covered. Total familiarity with the camera controls is essential using this method. Camouflage duct tape is available which is good for camouflaging cameras and other equipment. In lieu of camouflage tape, white medical tape can be used and coloured in with a black or brown texta pen or magic marker. The colours will be absorbed by the tape leaving a remarkably drab finish. The cassette ejection port, flip-out viewfinder and battery on a video camera must be kept clear when using tape. The same techniques can be used to camouflage portable radios, mini-tripods, night vision devices, binoculars and GPS receivers.

Shiny Objects

All shiny objects must be concealed or covered with tape. This includes watch faces, compasses and Swiss army knives.

Guidelines For Good Concealment

Good camouflage is an aid to concealment, however even the best camouflage will be wasted unless the operator remains conscious of why objects are seen and acts accordingly. Good concealment includes the rigid application of the following guidelines:

a. Look around or through concealment, not over it If there is no choice but to look over it, try to avoid breaking natural, straight lines.

b. The skyline is the worst background of all. If observing over cover and against the skyline, make use of something to break up the silhouette such as vegetation, rocks, etc. Avoid large bodies of water as they can have the same effect as skylines.

c. Use available shadow and remember that positions in the open may be compromised by the natural movement of the sun.

d. Choose a background which blends with the overall appearance of the terrain to avoid catching the eye of the target.

e. Avoid isolated cover. It is usually conspicuous and will attract attention.

f. Where possible, use covered routes when moving into or out of Observation Posts. A small dip in the ground or thick vegetation are ideal.

g. When movement is essential, move slowly and carefully.

Listed below are a number of additional hints which will assist in concealing the individual/s:

a. Use all available cover and concealment no matter whether it is natural or artificial. The use of vegetation, terrain and even man-made structures requires nothing more than common sense.

Avoid unnecessary movement and remember that fast movement attracts instant attention as does the sign the movement may leave. When movement is necessary, plan the move and then make it carefully, taking advantage of weather conditions such as wind and rain as well as artificial noise such as aircraft.

c. When taking up an observation position above ground outside the OP, try to use the prone position so that only a small part of your body is presented to the target.

d. Avoid moving across open areas

e. When stopping for a break, do not sit in the open, use available cover.

f. Do not openly expose anything that will shine such as cam paint case mirror, watch face, binoculars or lenses as the reflected shine may be seen from a long distance.

g. Drop no litter as this can lead to a compromise.

h. Any soil from digging OPs must be concealed.

i. Do not use torches or naked lights, strike matches or smoke cigarettes in the field.

j. Remember to treat NIGHT as DAY as the target may have access to commercially available night vision equipment

Camouflage is one of the most important skills in covert rural/remote area surveillance. When applied correctly and used in conjunction with the guidelines for good concealment, it enables the operator to produce effective intelligence products while maintaining the security of the operation and the safety of the operator.

Individual Daylight Movement

Each operator must know how to combine the art of concealment with movement. Different methods of movement provide concealment for different types of cover and these can be used by the operator when moving in the target area. The following points are important:

a. Before leaving a place of concealment, the next position to which it is intended to move and the best route to it should be selected.

b.   The movement of low foliage could attract attention by moving higher branches and leaves or by creating noise.

c.   Tall grass provides concealment, but movement through it may make it wave with an unnatural motion, thus attracting attention.

d.   After disturbing any animals or birds, remain still for a few minutes and observe.

e.   Take advantage of any distractions such as thunder, aircraft, etc to cover movement noise.

f.   Take advantage of fog, heavy rain, smoke or haze to assist in concealing movement.

g.   When moving to the OP position, be sure to halt every ten minutes or so for around one to two minutes and listen for any noise. This also tends to get the operator psychologically "in tune" with his or her environment.

A knowledge of how to move correctly and how to use ground for movement is important because:

a.   It enables operators and teams to close with the target without exposing themselves to detection.

b.   A knowledge of how to best move over ground assists a team to accomplish its task without detection.

c.   It enables an operator to occupy and leave a position without being observed by the target or other personnel in the area.

To assist in moving over ground the following methods of individual daylight movement have been developed:

a. The walk

b. The monkey run

c. The leopard crawl

d. The roll

The Walk

When moving in an area which is known to be close to the target, it is essential to walk silently and stealthily. The essential elements to be remembered when using the walk are to:

a. Move slowly and deliberately.

b. Lift the foot carefully and place it slowly and quietly in the next position.

c. Maintain the body in a balanced position at all times.

d. Keep the head up and observe in all directions, remembering that peripheral vision is sensitive to movement.

e. Always observe and note good cover and concealment positions while on the move.

f. Be continually alert and ready to rapidly move into concealment instantly if necessary.

g. Move very quietly on hard ground by placing the edge of the sole of the boot on the ground first.

h. Take great care to maintain balance when crossing obstacles so that a fall and therefore noise, is avoided.

The Monkey Run

The monkey run is basically crawling on hands and knees and is useful when moving behind low cover. The essential elements are:

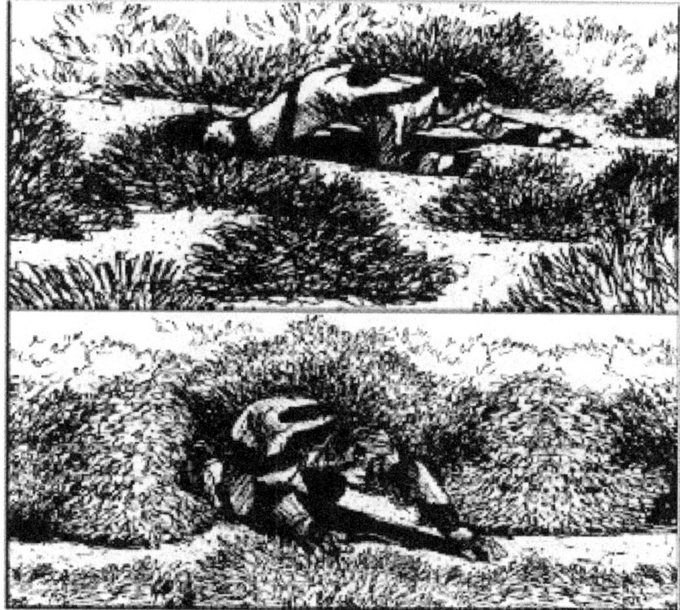

a. To reduce noise to a minimum, put the hands down in a place that is free of twigs or anything which may crack or rustle, then move the knees forward to the position where the hands have been.

b. Keep the buttocks and head low, but observe while advancing.

c. Movement can be quite fast but the faster the movement, the more noise will be generated.

d. Keep the length of pace short to reduce noise and discomfort.

The Leopard Crawl

The leopard crawl is crawling on the elbows and the inside of the knees. It is useful when moving behind very low cover. The essential elements of the leopard crawl are:

a. Movement is achieved by moving alternative elbows and knees, the body is rolled slightly as each knee is bent. (the same effect can be achieved by trailing one leg and using only one knee)

b. Keep the heels, head, body and elbows low down but observe while advancing.

The Roll

The roll is a very quick method of moving away from a position when it is known that the target has observed and is advancing towards the location. The essential element is that the arms and any equipment remain close to the side so that the body is almost circular and will roll quickly. In a threat environment (i.e an operation against a violent offender known to possess firearms), it may be good practise to do this every time you have to go to ground.

Tactical Route Selection

The skill of concealment and movement are combined when the operator is required to move from one point to another. To choose a route on which to move, look at the ground and decide on the following:

a.   Where to make for.

b.   The best route to get there

c.   Whether to walk, crawl, etc.

An ideal route is one which has:

a.   No significant obstacles

b.   Good cover to conceal the movement

c.   Places from which to observe without being detected
Unfortunately, these things seldom go together. While low ground is best for cover and concealment, high ground is best for observation.

Choose the best route according to the circumstances, plan the move and execute it according to plan. Continue moving in bounds, planning each in advance.

Stalking

The object of stalking is for the operator to move unseen to a position close to a moving or stationary target to ensure good quality photographs or video footage. The practical art of stalking incorporates the application of all aspects of fieldcraft, and is such that it can only be effectively learnt by repeated practice.

Any stalk undertaken without first doing a thorough reconnaissance is likely to have limited success. Opportunities to view the ground first hand may not be available, so maximum use of other sources such as maps and air photographs should be utilised. Topographical maps are available for most parts of Australia and some state government agencies have made large-scale aerial photographs available on the internet.

Before a stalk takes place, the following information should be considered in any reconnaissance:

a. *Estimated location of the target.* Particular attention should be given to nearby features and landmarks.

b. *The location of the OP.* The area that presents the best location for the OP should be identified, although the exact position can rarely be pinpointed in advance.

c. *Route selection.* The best route should be selected and split into bounds. Each bound can then be considered in greater detail as it is arrived at on the ground. Particular points to consider are as follows:

1. The availability of natural cover and any dead ground.

2. The position and frequency of any obstacles such as waterways and fences.

3. Likely "stop and listen" points along the route. Ideally, these should coincide with the start and finish of each bound.
4. The location of any other known or possible target or civilian locations.

5. The general method of movement, either crawling or walking, likely to be possible for each bound. This is important as it will dictate the time taken to move to the target area.

6. The extraction route should differ from that of the approach if at all possible, but should be planned in a similar manner.

To conduct a successful operation, much depends on the circumstances and the reactions to any emergency which may arise. The following should always be remembered:

a.   *Personal Camouflage.* Changes in local vegetation should be noted and any necessary alterations made to personal camouflage.

b.   *Direction.* Direction is best maintained if distant landmarks are used as guides to the target location.

c.   *Alertness.* Any relaxation in alertness could lead to detection by the target. Care must be taken at all times.

d.   *Observation.* Stop and listen with care at frequent intervals, especially at the start and end of each bound.

e.   *Exposure.* If surprised or exposed, instinctive reaction is necessary to either freeze in place or move quickly to the nearest cover away from the point of exposure.

f.   *Risks.* Take advantage of any local disturbances or distractions, which enable quicker movements than, would otherwise be possible. This involves a degree of risk and should not be attempted when close to the target.

g.   *Disturbed Wildlife.* The sudden departure of alarmed birds or animals from the area can draw the target's attention to the area of approach. Wait until the wildlife has settled down and check that the target's attention has not been drawn to that area.

Keeping Direction over Short Distances

The map and compass are the best means of keeping direction. When these aids are not available, the following methods can be used to help maintain direction:

a.   *Natural Features.* Nature provides many landmarks which may assist in maintaining direction such as rivers, streams and mountains. Selecting a landmark which is on the horizon and easily recognisable will allow direction to be maintained over quite long distances.

b.   *Using the Watch and Sun.* A non-digital wristwatch may be used as an improvised compass. Those watches with a rotating bezel are particularly useful. To find north, point the "12" at the sun. The point exactly halfway between the "12" and the hour hand is true north.

c.   *Using the stars.* Southern Cross is used to locate true south-north line. Draw an imaginary line between the Southern Cross and the two pointer stars. Drop an imaginary line from the halfway point between the Southern Cross and the Pointer Stars to the horizon. This is true south.

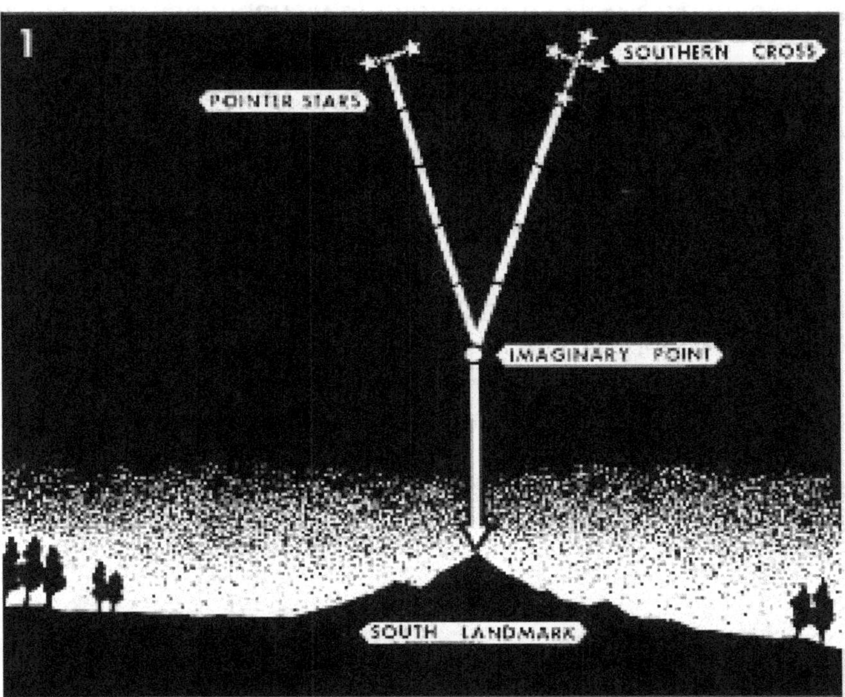

Night Observation

Darkness limits visibility, changes the outlines of objects, and distorts perceptions of distance. Dark objects seem farther away, while light ones seem closer. Therefore, orientation on the terrain and the detection and identification of objects is more difficult at night than during the day. Night observation is

conducted with the naked eye and, for particular applications, night vision devices.

Plan and organize night observation during the daylight period before the onset of darkness.

Techniques. Illegal activity is often conducted during the hours of darkness.

Some techniques for night observation are described below.

Dark adaptation. The exposure to light directly affects night vision. Repeated exposure to bright sunlight has an increasingly adverse effect on dark adaptation. Exposure to intense sunlight for 2 to 5 hours causes a definite decrease in visual sensitivity, which can persist for as long as 5 hours. This effect can be intensified by reflective surfaces such as sand and snow. At the same time, the rate of dark adaptation and degree of night vision capability are decreased. Since these effects are cumulative and may persist for several days, use polarised sunglasses or equivalent filter lenses in bright sunlight when night operations are anticipated.

Night vision scanning. Dark adaptation or night vision is only the frost step toward maximizing the ability to see at night. Night vision scanning can enable you to overcome many of the physiological vision limitations and can reduce the visual illusions that so often confuse the observers. The technique involves scanning from right to left or left to right using a slow, regular scanning movement. Although both day and night surveillance employ scanning movements, at night avoid looking directly at a faintly visible object when trying to confirm its presence.

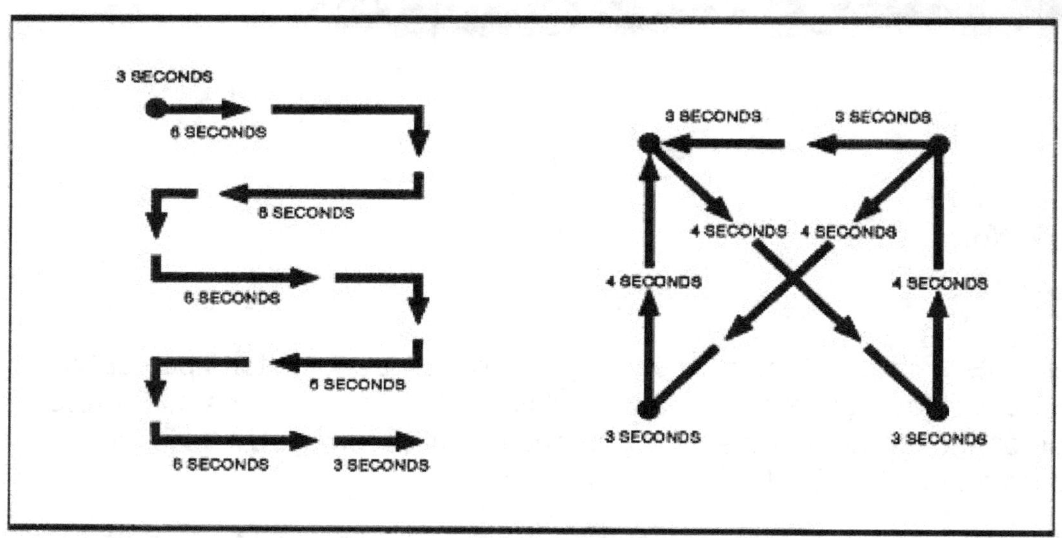

Night vision scanning techniques.

Use of off-center vision. Viewing an object using central vision during daylight poses no limitation, but this technique is ineffective at night. Limited night vision is due to the night blind spot that exists during periods of low illumination. To compensate for this limitation, use off-center vision. This technique requires you to view an object by looking 10 degrees above, below, or to either side of it, rather than directly at the object. This procedure allows the peripheral vision to maintain contact with an object.

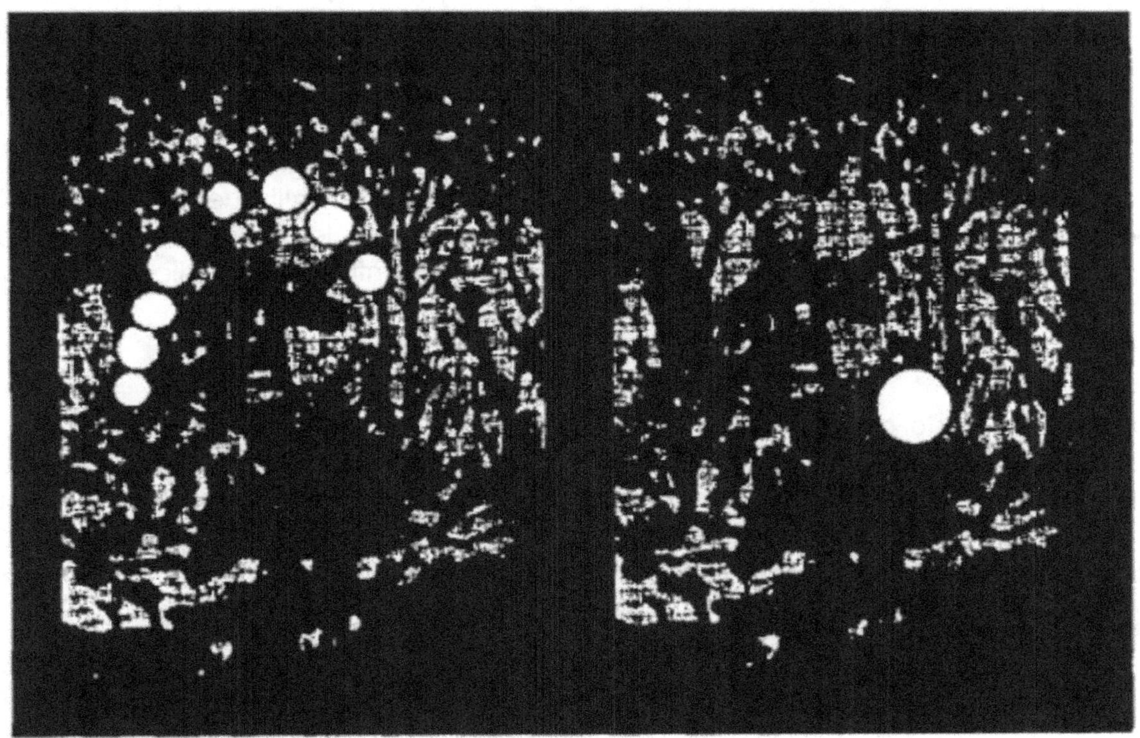

Off center viewing technique.

Countering the bleach-out effect. Even when off-center viewing is practiced, the image of an object viewed longer than 2 or 3 seconds tends to bleach out and become one solid tone. As a result, the object is no longer visible and can produce a potentially unsafe operating condition. To overcome this limitation, be aware of the phenomenon and avoid looking at an object longer than 2 or 3 seconds. By shifting your eyes from one off-center point to another, you can continue to pickup the object in your peripheral field of vision.

Shape or silhouette. The ability to visually make out shapes is significantly reduced at night; consequently, you must identify objects by their shape or silhouette. They must become familiar with the architectural design of structures, vehicles, equipment, and like objects, common to your Area of Operations to maximize information collection. Your success using this technique comes from extensive and practice.

Confidence. In order to gain confidence in the ability to see under low light levels, the correct use must be made of the eyes. The operator must believe what his or her eyes are telling them. Through practice, an operator must learn to recognise objects at night and know how they differ from their daytime appearance. This night time familiarity can only be obtained by constant practice. Once an operator is familiar with the techniques of seeing at night without night vision devices, the confidence necessary for night operations will quickly follow.

Protection of Night Vision. Any bright light will spoil night vision. It is important that the operator instinctively closes or covers one eye when faced with any light at night. In addition, he or she should:

a.   Avoid looking at any bright light unnecessarily.

b.   Shield the eyes from any bright light source such as vehicle headlights.

c.   Use red filters on torches to assist in maintaining night vision.

d.   Use only one eye when using Night Vision devices as the device will diminish night vision in the eye being used.

Night Movement

The target may be alert at night especially if he or she is conducting illegal activities. It is therefore important that the operator knows how to move at night without being detected and what action to take if caught in unexpected lights.

Darkness provides most of the concealment at night, but due to the proliferation of relatively cheap night vision equipment, night should be treated much the same as daylight.

To assist in remaining concealed in the dark, all equipment must be camouflaged and anything that may gleam in moonlight or show up on night vision devices must be covered.

To minimise the risk of making noise:

a.   Tie string around the trousers at the ankles, knees and thighs to prevent the cloth from making nose.

b.   Check that there are no rattles in your equipment

c.   Wear a soft hat or go bareheaded.

At night, more is heard than is seen, so silence is vital. To move silently at night, the operator has to move slowly. The correct selection of routes across country is vital so the best use is made of available concealment and cover. When selecting routes for night time movement, the following aids can be used either individually or combined:

a.   *Landmarks.* Ideally two prominent objects which are visible to the front at night are selected and are kept lined up in view. When one object alone is used, its position related to the target area is checked, that is left of, in line with, or right of. It is useful to have a landmark on the back view particularly if a return is necessary.

b.   *Pacing.* Operators should memorise the number of paces they require to cover a known distance, for example, 100m in different vegetation and on various terrains. Pace counters can be used to keep check on distance covered. These can be easily improvised by using a piece of string with knots at regular intervals.

c.   *Optical aids.* Optics such as binoculars provide a means of observation at least twice the limit of normal night vision and are also useful for viewing landmarks.

d.   *Compass.* The compass is the most reliable aid and should be used in conjunction with a map and air photographs. Bearings should be worked out by day.

Night Movement Techniques

Night movement demands more care than daylight movement and the basic night movement general rules should be applied as follows:

a.   At night, people hear more than they see, so silence is vital. To move silently at night, move slowly.

b.   Move by bounds, that is short distances at a time. Halt, look, listen, and then move again. Halt in cover or shadow if there is any. If there is not, then lie down. By lying down, the operator is unlikely to be sky lined and more things will be sky lined to him/her. Humans also hear better with their ears closer to the ground due to the general reduction in wind noise. If a suspicious noise is heard when moving it is usually best to freeze for a moment to look and listen, then slowly and silently take cover or lay down.

c.   Move in cleared areas as much as possible to avoid noise, but be aware that an observer may possess night vision equipment.

d.   Take advantage of sounds such as thunder, wind, aircraft, etc. to cover movement noise.

e.   Avoid running at night except when absolutely essential. Running increases noise and there is a risk of injury through falling over obstacles.

Night movement can be very slow and tiring. The following methods are used:

a.   *The walk.* The walk at night is described as follows:

1. Balance the weight on the rear foot. Raise the other leg high to clear any scrub or grass.

2. Place the side of the boot down first, then gently feel for a firm foothold free of twigs.

3. Transfer the weight carefully onto the forward foot.

b. *Crawling.* Night crawling is described as follows:

1. The monkey run is carried out as per the daytime technique.

2. The daytime leopard crawl is far too noisy for use at night. The crawl quietly at night:

    a. Lie on the stomach, legs together, arms extended about half-way forward.

    b. Gently clear the way ahead with the hands to clear twigs, leaves, etc.

    c. Reach forward with the toes, raise the body clear of the ground on the forearms and toes and carry it forward and gently to the ground again.

CHAPTER 4

TRACKING

When an operator follows a trail, he builds a picture of the enemy in his mind by asking himself questions:

How many persons am I following?

Are they Armed?

Are they healthy?

Are they tired?

Do they know they are being followed?

To answer these questions, the operator uses available indicators to track the enemy. The operator looks for signs that reveal an action occurred at a specific time and place. For example, a footprint in soft sand is an excellent indicator, since an operator can determine the specific time the person passed. By comparing indicators, the operator obtains answers to his questions. For example, a footprint and a waist-high scuff on a tree may indicate that an armed individual passed this way, scuffing the tree with his rifle butt.

Any indicator the operator discovers can be defined by one of five tracking concepts: displacement, weather, litter, camouflage, and immediate-use intelligence.

Displacement.

Displacement takes place when anything is moved from its original position. A well-defined footprint or shoe print in soft, moist ground is a good example of displacement. By studying the footprint or shoe print, the operator determines several important facts. For example, a print left by worn footgear or by bare feet may indicate lack of proper equipment. Displacement can also result from clearing a trail by breaking or cutting through heavy vegetation with a machete. These trails are obvious to the most inexperienced operator who is tracking. Individuals may unconsciously break more branches as they follow someone who is cutting the vegetation. Displacement indicators can also be made by persons carrying heavy loads who stop to rest; prints made by box edges can help to identify the load. When loads are set down at a rest halt or campsite, they usually crush grass and twigs. A reclining soldier also flattens the vegetation.

a.   *Analyzing Footprints.* Footprints may indicate direction, rate of movement, number, sex, and whether the individual knows he is being tracked.

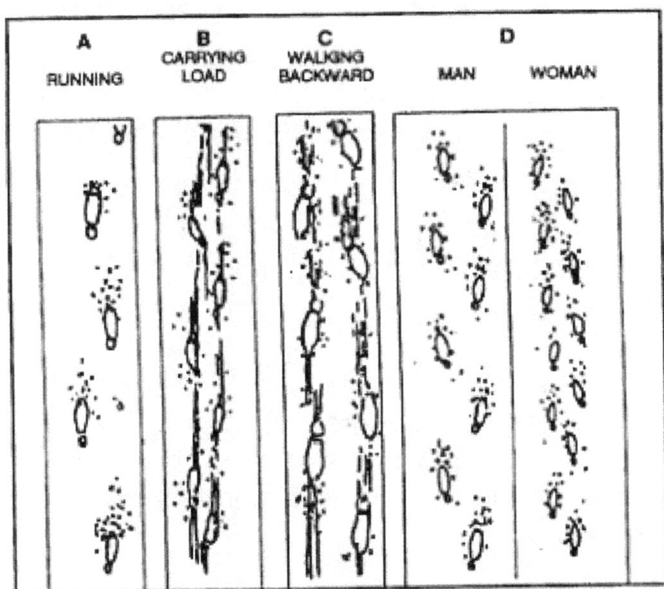

Figure 8-1. Different types of footprints.

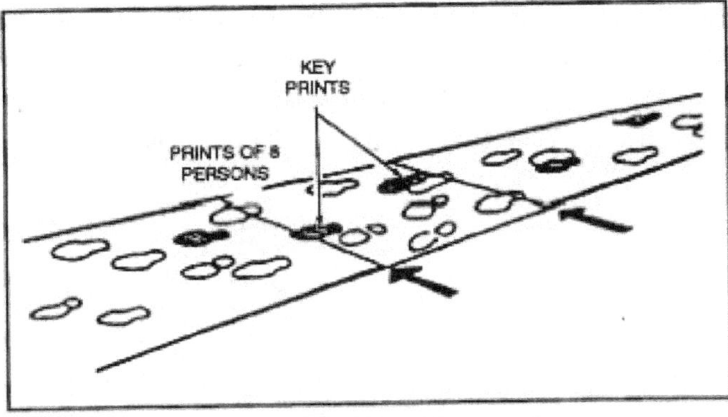

Figure 8-2. Stride measurement.

(1) If footprints are deep and the pace is long, rapid movement is

apparent. Long strides and deep prints with toe prints deeper than heel

prints indicate running.

(2) Prints that are deep, short, and widely spaced, with signs of scuffing or shuffling indicate the person is carrying a heavy load.

(3) If the party members realize they are being followed, they may try to hide their tracks.

Persons walking backward have a short, irregular stride. The prints have an unnaturally deep toe, and soil is displaced in the direction of movement.

(4) To determine the sex, the operator should study the size and position of the footprints. Women tend to be slightly pigeon-toed, while men walk with their feet straight ahead or pointed slightly to the outside. Prints left by women are usually smaller and the stride is usually shorter than prints left by men.

b.   *Determining Key Prints.* The last individual in the file usually leaves the clearest footprints; these become the key prints. The operator cuts a stick to match the length of the prints and notches it to indicate the width at the widest part of the sole. He can then study the angle of the key prints to the direction of march. The operator looks for an identifying mark or feature, such as worn or

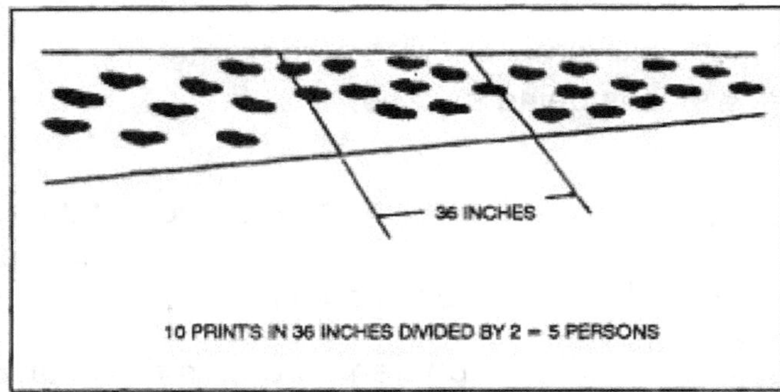

Figure 8-3. 36-Inch box method.

frayed footwear, to help him identify the key prints. If the trail becomes vague, erased, or merges with another, the operator can use his stick-measuring devices and, with close study, can identify the key prints. This method helps the operator to stay on the trail. A technique used to count the total number of individuals being tracked is the box method. There are two methods the operator can use to employ the box method.

(1)   The most accurate is to use the stride as a unit of measure when key prints can be determined. The operator uses the set of key prints and the edges of the road or trail to box in an area to analyze. This method is accurate under the right conditions for counting up to 18 persons.

(2)   The operator may also use the 36-inch box method if key prints are not evident. To use the 36-inch box method, the operator uses the edges of the road or trail as the sides of the box. He measures a cross section of the area 36 inches long, counting each indentation in the box and dividing by two. This method gives a close estimate of the number of individuals who made the prints; however, this system is not as accurate as the stride measurement.

c. *Recognizing Other Signs of Displacement*

Foliage, moss, vines, sticks, or rocks that are scuffed or snagged from their original position form valuable indicators. Vines may be dragged, dew droplets displaced, or stones and sticks overturned to show a different color underneath. Grass or other vegetation may be bent or broken in the direction of movement.

(1) The operator inspects all areas for bits of clothing, threads, or dirt from footgear that can be torn or can fall and be left on thorns, snags, or the ground.

(2) (2) Flushed from their natural habitat, wild animals and birds are another example of displacement. Cries of birds excited by unnatural movement is an indicator; moving tops of tall grass or shrubs on a windless day indicates that someone is moving the vegetation.

(3)

(3) Changes in the normal life of insects and spiders may indicate that someone has recently passed. Valuable clues are disturbed bees, ant holes uncovered by someone moving over them, or torn spin webs across open areas, spider webs. Spiders often trails, or roads to trap flying insects. If the tracked person does not avoid these webs, he leaves an indicator to an observant operator.

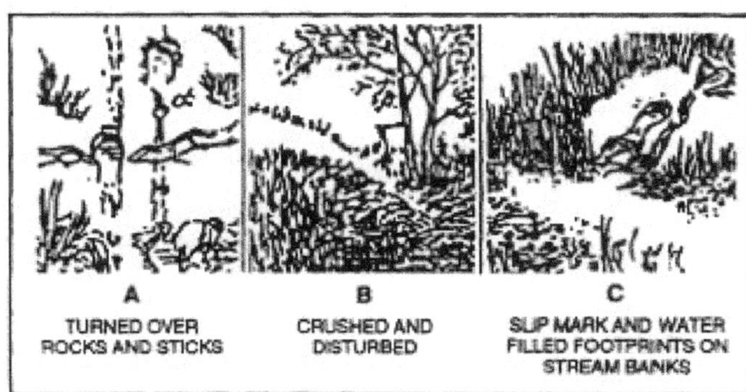

Figure 8-4. Other displacements.

(4) If the person being followed tries to use a stream to cover his trail, the operator can still follow successfully. Algae and other water plants can be displaced by lost footing or by careless walking. Rocks can be displaced from their original position or overturned to indicate a lighter or darker color on the opposite side. The person entering or exiting a stream creates slide marks or footprints, or scuffs the bark on roots or sticks. Normally, a person or animal seeks the path of least resistance; therefore, when searching the stream for an indication of departures, operators will find signs in open areas along the banks.

WEATHER

Weather either aids or hinders the operator. It also affects indicators in certain ways so that the operator can determine their relative ages. However, wind, snow, rain, or sunlight can erase indicators entirely and hinder the operator. The operator should know how weather affects soil, vegetation, and other indicators in his area. He cannot determine the age of indicators until he understands the effects that weather has on trail signs.

a. By studying weather effects on indicators, the operator can determine the age of the sign (for example, when bloodstains are fresh, they are bright red). Air and sunlight first change blood to a deep ruby-red color, then to a dark brown crust when the moisture evaporates. Scuff marks on trees or bushes darken with time; sap oozes, then hardens when it makes contact with the air.

b. Weather affects footprints. By carefully studying the weather process, the operator can estimate the age of the print. If particles of soil are beginning to fall into the print, the operator should become a stalker. If the edges of the print are dried and crusty, the prints are probably about one hour old. This varies with terrain and should be considered as a guide only.

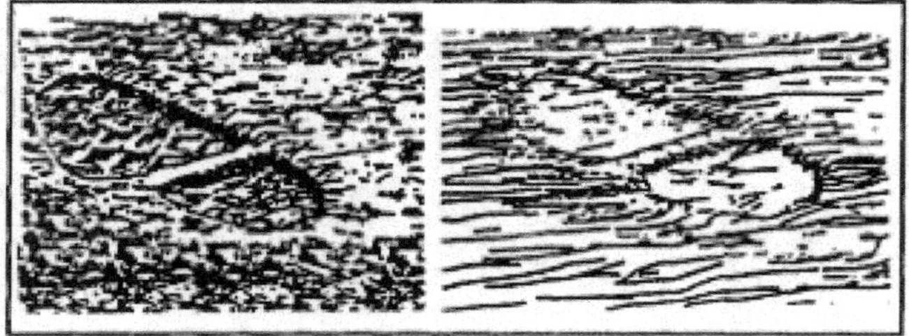

Figure 8-5. Weather effects on footprints.

c. A light rain may round the edges of the print. By remembering when the last rain occurred, the operator can place the print into a time frame. A heavy rain may erase all signs.

d. Trails exiting streams may appear weathered by rain due to water running from clothing or equipment into the tracks. This is especially true if the party exits the stream single file. Then, each person deposits water into the tracks. The existence of a wet, weathered trail slowly fading into a dry trail indicates the trail is fresh.

e. Wind dries tracks and blows litter, sticks, or leaves into prints.

By recalling wind activity, the operator may estimate the age of the tracks.

For example, the operator may reason "the wind is calm at the present but blew hard about an hour ago. These tracks have litter in them, so they must be over an hour old." However, he must be sure that the litter was not crushed into them when the prints were made.

(1) Wind affects sounds and odors. If the wind is blowing toward the operator, sounds and odors may be carried to him; conversely, if the wind is blowing *away* from the operator, he must be extremely cautious since wind also carries sounds toward the enemy. The operator can determine wind direction by dropping a handful of dust or dried grass from shoulder height. By pointing in the same direction the wind is blowing, the operator can localize sounds by cupping his hands behind his ears and turning slowly. When sounds are loudest, the operator is facing the origin.

(2) In calm weather (no wind), air currents that may be too light to detect can carry sounds to the operator. Air cools in the evening and moves downhill toward the valleys. If the operator is moving uphill late in the day or at night, air currents will probably be moving toward him if no other wind is blowing. As the morning sun warms the air in the valleys, it moves uphill. The operator considers these factors when plotting patrol routes or other operations. If he keeps the wind in his face, sounds and odors will be carried to him from his objective or from the party being tracked.

LITTER

A poorly trained or poorly disciplined group moving over terrain may leave a trail of litter. Unmistakable signs of recent movement are gum or candy wrappers, food cans, cigarette butts, remains of fires, or human feces. Rain flattens or washes litter away and turns paper into pulp. Exposure to weather can cause food cans to rust at the opened edge; then, the rust moves toward the center. The operator must consider weather conditions when estimating the age of litter. He can use the last rain or strong wind as the basis for a time frame.

CAMOUFLAGE

Camouflage applies to tracking when the followed party employs techniques to baffle or slow the operator. For example, walking backward to leave confusing prints, brushing out trails, and moving over rocky ground or through streams.

IMMEDIATE-USE INTELLIGENCE

The operator combines all indicators and interprets what he has seen to form a composite picture for on-the-spot intelligence. For example, indicators may show contact with the target is imminent and require extreme stealth.

a. The operator avoids reporting his interpretations as facts. He reports what he has seen rather than stating these things exist. There are many ways an operator can interpret the sex and size of the party, the load, and the type of equipment. Timeframes can be determined by weathering effects on indicators.

b. Immediate-use intelligence is information about the target that can be used to gain surprise, to keep him off balance, or to keep him from escaping the area entirely. The team may have many sources of intelligence reports, documents, or informants. These sources can be combined to form indicators of the target's last location, future plans, and destination.

CHAPTER 5

COUNTERTRACKING

If a highly alert target with excellent local area knowledge and some tracking experience finds the tracks of two men, this may indicate that a highly trained team may be operating in the area. However, a knowledge of countertracking enables the team to avoid compromise by remaining undetected.

EVASION

Evasion of the tracker or pursuit team is a difficult task that requires the use of immediate-action drills to counter the threat. A team skilled in tracking techniques can successfully employ deception drills to lessen signs that the enemy can use against them. However, it is very difficult for a person, especially a group, to move across any area without leaving signs noticeable to the trained eye.

CAMOUFLAGE

The team may use the most used and the least used routes to cover its movement. It also loses travel time when trying to camouflage the trail.

    a.   **Most Used Routes.** Movement on lightly traveled sandy or soft trails is easily tracked. However, an operator may try to confuse the tracker by moving on hard-surfaced, often-traveled roads or by merging with civilians. These routes should be carefully examined; if a well-defined approach leads to the target's camp, it may be boobytrapped, ambushed, or covered by security devices.

b.   **Least Used Routes.** Least used routes avoid all man-made trails or roads and confuse the tracker. These routes are normally magnetic bearings between two points. However, the tracker can use the proper concepts to follow the team if he is experienced and persistent.

c.   **Reduction of Trail Signs.** An operator who tries to hide his trail moves at reduced speed; therefore, the experienced tracker gains time. Common methods to reduce trail signs areas follows:

1) Wrap footgear with rags or wear soft-soled sneakers, which make footprints rounded and leas distinctive.

(2) Brush out the trail. This is rarely done without leaving signs.

(3) Change into footgear with a different tread pattern following a deceptive maneuver.

(4) Walk on hard or rocky ground.

DECEPTION TECHNIQUES

Evading a skilled and persistent tracker requires skillfully executed maneuvers to deceive the tracker and to cause him to lose the trail. A tracker cannot be outrun by a team that is carrying equipment, because he travels light and may be supported by comrades with vehicle or even light aircraft support. The size of the pursuing force dictates the team's chances of success in employing ambush-type maneuvers. Teams use some of the following techniques in immediate-action drills and deception drills.

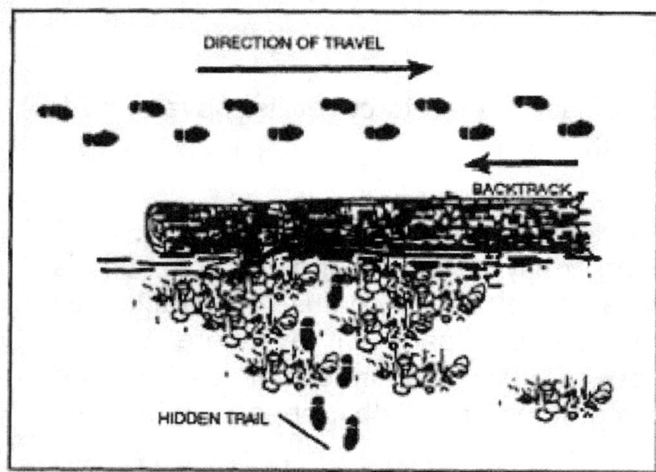

Figure 8-6. Walking backward.

a. **Backward Walking.** One of the basic techniques used is that of walking backward (Figure 8-6) in tracks already made, and then stepping off the trail onto terrain or objects that leave little sign. Skillful use of this maneuver causes the tracker to look in the wrong direction once he has lost the trail.

b. **Large Tree** A good deception tactic is to change directions at large trees (Figure 8-7). To do this, the operator moves in any given direction and walks past a large tree (12 inches wide or larger) from 5 to 10 paces. He carefully walks backward to the forward side of the tree and makes a 90-degree change in the direction of travel, passing the tree on its forward side. This technique uses the tree as a screen to hide the new trail from the pursuing tracker.

NOTE: By studying signs, a tracker may determine if an attempt is being made to confuse him. If the team loses the tracker by walking backward, footprints will be deepened at the toe and soil will be scuffed or dragged in the direction of movement. By following carefully the tracker can normally find a turnaround point.

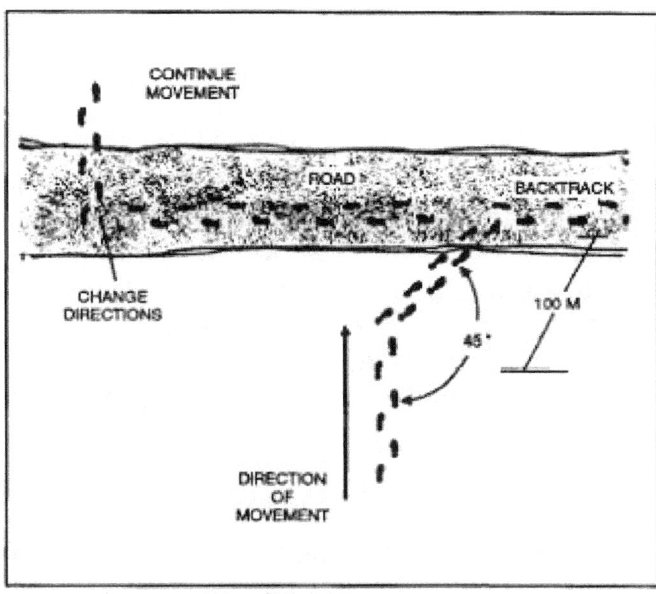

Figure 8-8. Cut the corner.

c. **Cut the Corner.** Cut-the-corner technique is used when approaching a known road or trail. About 100 meters from the road, the team changes its direction of movement, either 45 degrees left or right. Once the road is reached, the team leaves a visible trail in the same direction of the deception for a short distance on the road. The tracker should believe that the team "cut the corner" to save time. The team backtracks on the trail to the point where it entered the road, and then it carefully moves on the road without leaving a good trail.

Once the desired distance is achieved, the team changes direction and continues movement (Figure 8-8).

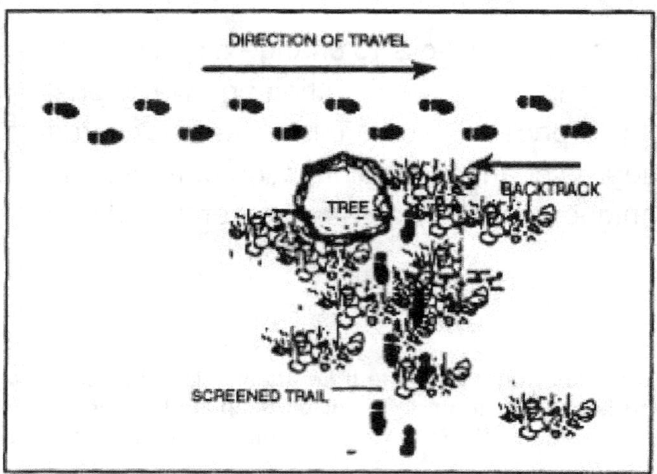

Figure 8-7. Large tree.

d. **Slip the Stream.** The team uses slip-the-stream technique when approaching a known stream. The team executes this method the same as the cut the comer technique. The team establishes the 45-degree deception maneuver upstream, then enters the stream. The team moves upstream to prevent floating debris and silt from compromising its direction of travel, and the team establishes false trails upstream if time permits. Then, it moves downstream to escape since creeks and streams gain tributaries that offer more escape alternatives.

f. **Fishhook.** The team uses the fishhook technique to double back on its own trail in an overwatch position. The team can observe the back trail for trackers or ambush pursuers.

CHAPTER 6

<u>RURAL OBSERVATION POST SITING AND CONSTRUCTION</u>

Observation Post Sites

When conducting surveillance, the team leader reconnoiters and selects a hide position and a surveillance position. The two positions can be in the same location. This decision is based on an estimate of the situation. The hide site provides a base from which to stage HF or satellite communications (either a remote communication site or directly from the hide site). It also reduces the number of personnel at the surveillance site, thereby reducing the chance of compromise.

The hide site provides an operational base for the team from which personnel can be rotated to and from the surveillance site. The surveillance site is where selected team members observe or survey the objective. Communication between the two sites is by wire, FM, or messenger.

TYPES OF HIDE AND SURVEILLANCE SITES

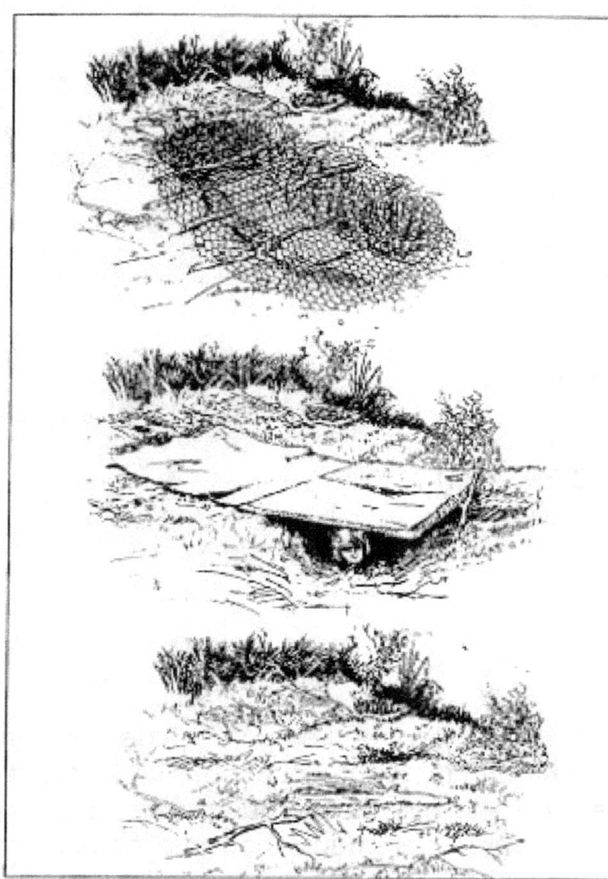

Figure E-1. One-man surface site.

The type of hide or surveillance site employed depends on conditions on site. Improvement of camouflage, at a minimum, must be continuous while occupying the site. The situation may not allow a team to improve from a surface site to a subsurface site.

a. **Surface Site.**

(1) *Advantages.*

Easy to construct.

Requires minimal materials. Can be done quickly and quietly. No large amounts of soil need to be relocated.

Stand-off capable optics are used to provide the security that is lost due to less camouflage.

Surveillance team can escape quickly.

(2) *Disadvantages.*

Little protection from weapons fire.

Risk of compromise by dogs and civilians.

(3) *Construction materials.*
Poncho(s) (waterproof).

Yetti or camouflage net. (Prevents reflection of poncho; aids in camouflage.) 550-pound cord or bungee cord.

Chicken wire (optional).

Burlap or canvas cloth (optional).

(4) *Considerations for surface site.*

(a) Team members avoid cutting any vegetation. They use man-made or natural camouflage.

(b) Team members keep all equipment packed when not in use.

(c) Team members always stay in uniform. They do not remove load-carving equipment.

(d) Security is maintained 24 hours a day.

(e) Two to three team members may occupy a surveillance site. With three team members, they can stay longer, and one team member can rest.

However, the site is larger and harder to conceal.

(f) The best time to switch surveillance teams is just after dark and just before daylight.

(g) Communication is setup between the hide site and the surveillance site.

(h) Team members take rucksacks to the surveillance site.

(i) In some situations, surveillance of the objective may only be done during limited visibility; the team stays in the hide site during the day.

(j) The surveillance site has all-round coverage, with nets or natural camouflage so it cannot be seen from any angle to include overhead.
(k) Distance between the hide site, the surveillance site, and the communication site (if used) depends on site conditions. Terrain should be the main factor.

(1) The team changes directions when moving from the hide site to the surveillance site, when possible (dog leg, fish hook, or indirect route).

(m) The team does not wear camouflage sniper suits (at least two per team) during movement. Pieces of the suit will rip off in vegetation and leave a trail. The operators put the suits on just before occupying the surveillance site.

b. **Hasty Subsurface Site.** A hasty subsurface site is constructed when there is not enough time to construct a complete subsurface site. The site is especially useful when there is little natural cover and concealment. The site is planned so that it can be improved to a full subsurface site as time and the situation allows.

(1) *Advantages.*

Lower profile than surface surveillance site.

Excellent camouflage.

(2) *Disadvantages.*

Limited construction tools. Soil must be concealed. Requires more time to construct. Construction noise.

(3) *Construction materials.*

Ponchos or other waterproofing. Yetti net or small camouflage net to assist in camouflage.

Entrenching tool.

550-pound cord or bungee cord.
Chicken wire (optional).

Burlap or canvas (optional).
Sandbags.

PVC pipe with connectors.
Fiberglass rod.

Aluminum conduit.
Plywood.

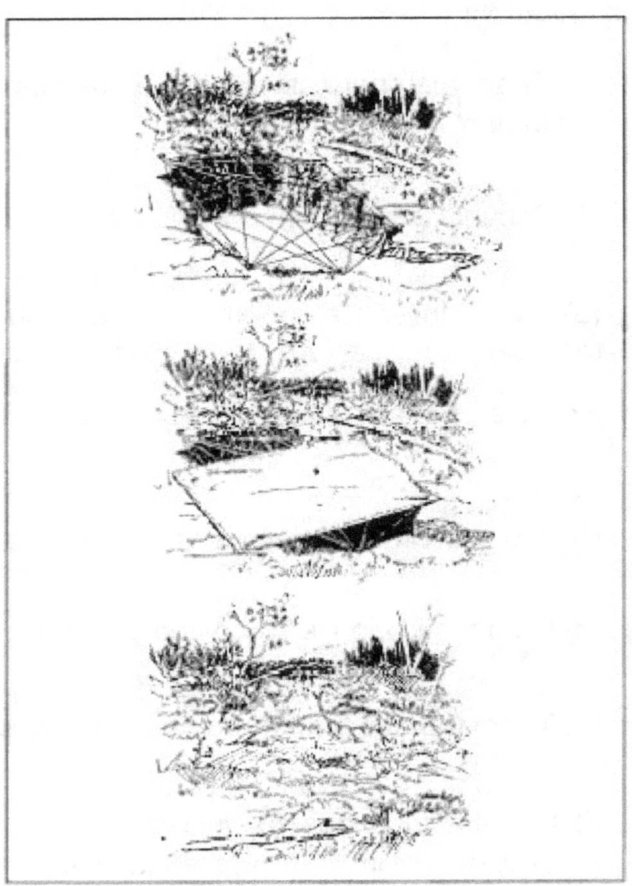

Figure E-2. Suspension line weaved site.

c. **Subsurface Site.** Teams will be underground for a long time. The site must be large enough to accommodate the entire team. The site should be dug in a well-concealed area, away from observation. The site may be dug and stocked with rations, water, batteries, and so on. Equipment, such as rucksacks and communications equipment, should be arranged so that a fast exit can be made in an emergency. A primary entrance and exit and an emergency entrance and exit should be built in the hide site.

If someone should find the primary entrance, some type of deception should be made at that entrance and the emergency exit should be used. The team should have an SOP for leaving a subsurface site. If surveillance is done from the site, leaving the site depends on where the site is in relation to the objective or on the terrain in which it is located.

Figure E-3. PVC site.

The site must have enough room for the team to move around freely.

The entrance and exits are covered and concealed.

The top of the site should be strong enough so that personnel can walk on it.

Dirt is removed from the site in rucksacks, sandbags, socks, or anything that can be used as a container. Most of the dirt is placed back on the top.

The team camouflages the leftover dirt.

They look for natural depressions, remove the top cover, fill in the depression, and recamouflage, or use streams or waterways during heavy rains.

They avoid populated areas as much as possible.

The team camouflages the site during construction by using yetti nets with camouflage material, natural camouflage, or chicken wire with camouflage material.

The team removes waste by using ziplock bags or anything that can be used as a container.

They can use a cardboard box with a bin liner bag as a toilet or a portable camping toilet. They have a bag of lime or baking soda to cover the odor.

(1) *Advantages.*

Little risk of compromise.

Excellent camouflage.

(2) *Disadvantages.*

Requires considerable time to construct.

Soil must be concealed away from the site.

Construction noise. Manpower, material, and equipment required to construct.

(3) *Construction materials (dependent on design).*

Fifty 2-inch by 4-inch by 12-foot boards; six 4-inch by 4-inch by 6-foot boards.

Gravel to cover floor. Eighteen inches of overhead cover over entire site.

Backhoe or personnel with shovels.

One-hundred

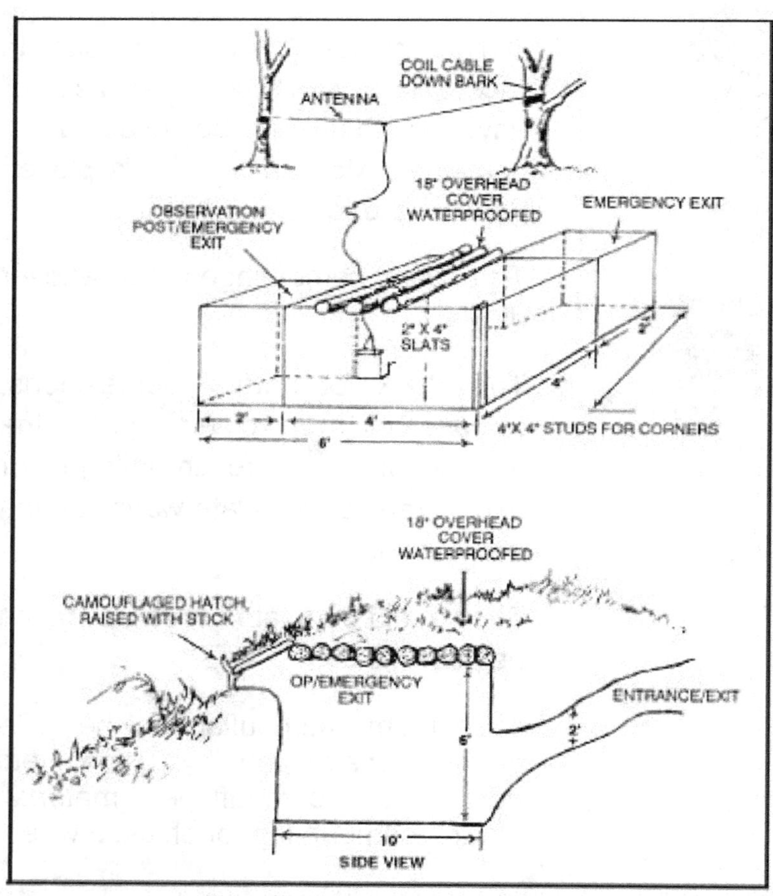

Figure E-4. Example of subsurface site.

sandbags. General-purpose large tent to cover digging operations until complete.

SITE SELECTION CONSIDERATIONS

When selecting an OP site, the leader should consider the following aspects:

Line of sight to target.

Within a range that can be supported by available observation equipment to meet the reporting requirements.

Overhead concealment and cover.

Away from natural lines of drift.

Away from roads, trails, railroad tracks, and major waterways.

Primary and alternate hasty exits.

Concealed serviceable entrance; little noise getting into and out of the hide site.

Not near man-made objects.

Downwind of inhabited areas.

Not dominated by high ground, but takes advantage of the high ground.

LEADER'S RECONNAISSANCE

The team leader initially selects the tentative sites during the planning phase. He selects the sites by physical reconnaissance, aerial observation, photographs, line -of-site data, soil and drainage data, or map reconnaissance. At a minimum, the team leader selects primary and alternate hide sites, and primary and alternate surveillance sites. Before the team occupies the sites, the team leader conducts a physical reconnaissance of the tentative site chosen during planning. If necessary, the team leader moves the site to a better location.

OCCUPATION OF THE HIDE SITE

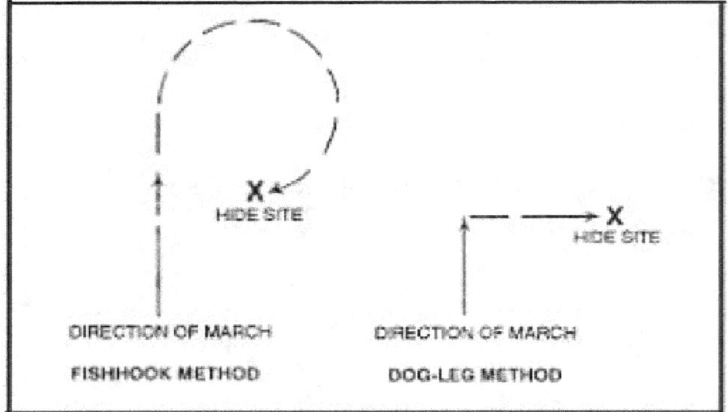

Figure E-5. Fishhook and dog-leg methods.

When occupying the hide site, the team leader has several methods he can select, however the most secure and effective method is detailed below

Fishhook or Dog-Leg Method. These methods are done from the direction of march.

ACTIONS IN THE HIDE SITE

The team maintains security at all times. Team members are positioned either back-to-back or feet-to-feet, using all-round security.

a. The team waits 15 minutes before moving or unpacking equipment, using time as a listening halt. They do not lean against small trees or vegetation.

b. If HF communication is to be conducted from the hide site, the antenna is constructed before dark. The antenna is not raised off the ground until communication is established. This reduces the amount of noise and movement at night.

c. Team members wear their load-carrying equipment at all times. They camouflage all-round the position.

d. The best time to rotate teams is at dusk and dawn. The surveillance team takes their rucksacks. The team rests during the day.

PRIORITY OF WORK

Work priorities may vary, with the exception of security. The team has security, alert, evacuation, and rendezvous plans. The team conducts stand-to starting before first light and continue it until after full light. They conduct stand-to starting before dark and continue it until after dark. They vary the starting times to keep from setting a pattern. They select and reconnoiter alternate hide and surveillance sites. They maintain equipment, radios, and camouflage. They ensure to perform personal hygiene and preventive medicine. They have a meal plan. They prepare guard and rest plans.

SITE STERILIZATION

Before departing hide and surveillance locations, team members must ensure sites and routes have been sterilized.

a. Personnel carry out all foreign debris.

b. If possible, they do not bury waste or rubbish. Animals will uncover rubbish or waste and expose it. If trash is buried, the team buries it 18 to 24 inches deep in sealed containers or covers the scent by using lime.

c. The team sterilizes the sites using displaced earth. They use the site to bury overhead material, which contrasts with the surrounding area.

d. The team camouflages the area by blending the site with local surroundings. e. As team members withdraw from the site, they ensure routes are camouflaged to prevent detection.

CHAPTER 7

NON-COVERT SUPPORT VEHICLE OPERATIONS

The purpose of a support vehicle is to provide transportation, resupply, communications and even shelter to the rural surveillance or OP team during operations. A non-covert support vehicle may be used when the target area is reasonably accessible by vehicle and there is a fair amount of other traffic. In this situation, a conventional vehicle with a caravan or camper trailer would be ideal.

Terrain and Vegetation dictates the type of vehicle you will be able to use in the area of operation. If you are required to use transportation in remote areas, the first consideration in relation to terrain and vegetation is whether you require a 4WD vehicle.

For example, if you were required to transport personnel into and out of an area of operation such as Far North Queensland, a 2WD vehicle would be totally unsuitable. Poor quality dirt roads and flooded creeks are hazards that are inherent to that area. A 4WD or a quad all terrain motorcycle (depending on the needs) would be more suitable.

The vehicle utilized by the target should also be considered by the surveillance team. If the target is driving a 4WD then there is a real expectation that he/she will go off- road. Conversely, if the target utilises a 2WD vehicle, this lessens the probability that he is going to drive into an area where the terrain and vegetation is unsuitable for 2WD use.

Other vehicle concerns include:

Care should be taken when hiring a 4WD for surveillance activities. Hire vehicles are often registered in a different state to the area of operation (eg: Tasmanian registration in NSW). This means that the number plates will stand out in a remote location and will draw attention to your covert activities.

Vehicle tire tracks can alert the target /associates to the fact that there are other people in the area of operation. It is important, when using a vehicle, to use existing used dirt tracks where possible. If you need to travel cross-country to get to a remote area, you should consider the trail you are leaving and the obvious security implications. The ideal situation is to identify vehicle access into the area of operation that is not used by the people under surveillance.

Vehicles can be difficult to hide depending on the type of terrain and vegetation in the area of operation. Most 4WD's are large in size and have a number of reflective surfaces (eg: windows, rear vision mirrors, wheel hubs, etc) that can attract interest. You should consider carrying some hessian cloth, shade cloth (comes in both dark green and beige), military camouflage net or even a tarpaulin to camouflage the vehicle. Even something as simple as smearing mud over the surface of the vehicle can be effective in blending into the landscape.

Refueling can be a prime concern if you are required to travel long distances over rugged terrain. You need to plan the estimated fuel consumption of the vehicle against the types of terrain you will be negotiating (eg normal roads will give you good fuel economy. Driving over long stretches of soft sand (high revs) will give you poor fuel economy. You need to consider carrying extra fuel on the vehicle or identify and plan fuelling sites.

CHAPTER 8

COVERT RURAL/REMOTE AREA VEHICLE SURVEILLANCE

The object of covert vehicle surveillance is to follow a target's movements by vehicle and to deploy dismounted surveillance/OP personnel in remote areas and private property.

The success of the mission and survival of a covert surveillance vehicle team (SVT) in a high-risk area may lie in its ability to infiltrate, move, conduct surveillance operations, and exfiltrate—all without being detected. In covert rural vehicle surveillance operations, success of the operation survival depends upon moving solely at night and using proper camouflage measures during the day.

The ultimate Covert Remote Area Surveillance Vehicle? An Army 6WD Landrover with dirt bike as used by NORFORCE and Special Forces.

PLANNING CONSIDERATIONS

Ground Infiltration and Exfiltration. A vehicle leaves a unique signature such as tracks and noise that makes it difficult to conceal. Take extreme care during route selection. Other planning considerations are—

Rigging Vehicle. A common mistake is to take everything except the kitchen sink when using the SV. Take care to properly load and configure the vehicles for a long distance movement.

Trailer(s). These can be taken for use en route or cached.

TACTICAL VEHICLE MOVEMENT

When planning and conducting movement, consider the below listed fundamentals of movement to reduce chance of detection by the target.

Cover and Concealment

Use terrain features and vegetation that offer protection from observation. When using cover and concealment to its full advantage, a trade-off usually exists between security and speed of movement.

Skylining

Avoid skylining. Select routes that avoid high ground that may silhouette the vehicle.

Chokepoints

Avoid chokepoints. Chokepoints or areas where the terrain naturally channels routes are often sites for ambushes or areas that an alert target may have under observation. If a chokepoint proves impossible to avoid, then reconnoiter it thoroughly before moving through it.

Populated Areas

Avoid known or suspected populated areas. In arid areas, this means all water holes because the populace and therefore the target know all water holes. A surveillance vehicle team cannot move covertly if people know they are in the area.

Movement Discipline

Practice movement discipline. Movement discipline means adhering to your light, noise, litter, and interval rules. It also means keeping your speed slow enough so that you do not leave a large dust signature (usually 25 to 40 kilometres per hour on most surfaces at night, slower during the day).

Security

Maintain 360-degree security at all times to avoid being taken by surprise. The team operations leader and/or the unit SOP assigns a sector of observation to each member of the SV team during movement and at halts.

Routes and Contingencies

Make sure all team members know the route and contingency plans. This is especially important when more than one SVT is deployed to cover the same target

METHODS OF TRAVEL

There are two methods of travel in the operational area. They are either on existing tracks, trails, or roads, or traveling off-road or cross-country. There are advantages and disadvantages to both.

Trails/Tracks

Advantages are speed of movement, hard packed trails do not easily yield readable prints and signs of passage, quietness of movement, less stress on vehicles and tires, and navigation is sometimes easier.

Disadvantages are usually a greater chance of being seen or compromised, and natural lanes of observation exist for the target.

Cross-Country

Advantages in traveling off-road are there is less chance of observation or compromise, usually afford more cover and concealment, and there is less chance of an ambush by a well-prepared target.

Disadvantages are slower rates of movement, more noticeable vehicle tracks and signs of passage, tire failure and vehicle stress is greater, and navigation is usually more difficult. Some desert terrain is so rough that even a 4WD has trouble traversing it faster than a man can walk. It is vital that the SVT rehearses cross-country movement in terrain as close as possible to that of the target area before deployment.

ACTIONS AT HALTS

Any time the SVT conducts a planned halt (short or long), it will conduct a coordinated shutdown of all vehicles. The team leader initiates the shutdown using hand and arm signals. He exits his vehicle and stands where he can be seen by all the vehicles. He then waves his arm in a circle over his head and drops it toward the ground to signal all vehicles to shut down their engines at the same time. He uses the same procedure, when the halt is over, to start their engines at the same time. If it is not possible for the team leader to visually signal all the vehicles at the same time, he can use the radio to indicate engine shutdown or engine on. Use of the radio should be avoided to lessen the team's radio signature, but it can be conducted safely if done properly.

Once the vehicles have been shut down, the SVT conducts a security listening halt before any other functions take place. The length of time for the halts will be established in planning and/or by Team SOP.

Short-duration halts are used to communicate with higher headquarters, make necessary repairs, or establish a position fix. For halts of less than 15 minutes, the Team does not break travel formation. Personnel establish 360-degree security.

LAAGER SITES

Laager sites or remain all day (RAD) sites are vehicular patrol bases where mounted Teams can maintain their vehicles, rest their crews, plan missions, and hide during daylight. There are two types of laager sites: short duration (occupied for only one period of daylight) or long duration (occupied for longer than one period of daylight).

During route planning, select tentative primary and alternate laager sites on the primary and alternate routes. The Team should arrive in the general area of the laager sites about two hours before morning nautical twilight. This arrival time will allow enough time for a proper recon of the area and to emplace and camouflage the vehicles before first light.

Upon reaching a tentative laager site, or before first light, the motorcycle element or a dismounted element can reconnoiter it. Once selected, the team Leader and primary navigator enter the site on foot and direct the incoming vehicles into position. As each vehicle is placed into position, its members are assigned their area of responsibility.

After the team is in place, it conducts a listening period to determine if there is any activity in the area. Tasks, in order of priority, after the listening period are:

Ensure 100% security.

Launch a dismounted patrol to erase vehicle signs into the laager site for a predetermined distance set by the Team Leader.

Camouflage vehicles (one per section, the other provides security).

Establish observation posts (OPs) or listening posts (LPs), if necessary.

Establish field telephone communications to each vehicle.

Reduce security, refuel, perform maintenance, and attend to personal hygiene.

The laager site does not necessarily resemble a circle. The terrain and vegetation play a role in locating each vehicle. All vehicles may be placed in the perimeter if necessary, but normally the Leader's vehicle is located in the center of the laager site.

When selecting and preparing a laager site, the priority is concealment, remaining undetected, and if compromised, breaking contact rapidly. The Team camouflages and positions its vehicles with this thought in mind .

The team may have to occupy the laager site for more than one period of daylight. Such an occupation is most common when the team needs to wait for more advantageous weather or light conditions before moving, has deployed an OP team on a mission and must remain in the area, or in a situation where extensive repairs must be made before resuming the mission. When occupied for more than one period of daylight, additional tasks include—

Enhancing early warning measures such as perimeter alarms and other sensors.

Conducting reconnaissance and establishing surveillance of the area. Upon vacating the laager site, the team sterilizes the site as much as possible. Terrain limitations may not allow positioning of the team with multiple bug-out routes and still properly conceal the vehicles. Give priority to concealing the vehicles, even if it reduces the Team's potential evacuation routes.

Surveillance Vehicle Camouflage

A well-camouflaged SVT in an arid area

SVTs operating in remote areas will have to stay undetected by local civilians, landowners, tourists, recreational four wheel drivers and motocross riders as well as the target to complete the operation. As most SVT operations will be unsupported and in remote areas, the only way to remain undetected is using proper camouflage measures. The Team's ability to hide in a remote area is limited only by the imagination and resourcefulness of its members.

VEHICLE CAMOUFLAGE THEORY

The biggest threat to the Team is detection. Detection can be by—

Direct observation.

Where the observer sees the subject with his eyes, either aided or unaided.

Indirect observation. Where the observer sees an image of the subject and not the subject itself. Indirect observation uses photography, infrared, thermal imaging, and video.

Regardless of the method of observation, certain factors help the eye and brain identify an object. The six factors of recognition are—

Position. This factor relates to the position of the object in relation to its surroundings. In addition, position is space relative to one object and another.

Shape. Experience teaches people to associate an object with its shape or outline. At a distance, the outline of objects can be recognized long before the details of its makeup can be determined. Trucks, guns, tanks, and other common military items all have distinctive outlines that help to identify them.

Shadow. Shadow may be even more revealing than the object itself. This fact is true when viewed from the air. Sometimes it may be more important to break up or disrupt the shadow than the object itself.

Texture. Texture refers to the ability of an object to reflect, absorb, and diffuse light. It may be defined as the relative smoothness or roughness of a surface. A rough surface reflects little light and will usually appear dark to the eye or in a photo. A smooth surface such as an airstrip, although it might be painted the same color as its surroundings, would show up as a lighter tone on a photo. One of the most revealing breaches of camouflage discipline is shine. Shine attracts attention by reflecting light such as sunlight or moonlight.

Contrast. Color is an aid to an observer when there is a contrast between the object and its background. The greater the contrast in color, the more visible the object is. Usually darker shades of a given color will be less likely to attract an observer's attention than the lighter shades.

Movement. The last factor of recognition is movement. Although this factor seldom reveals the identity of an object, it is the most important one of revealing location. Movement is detected easily and usually through the observer's peripheral vision.

CAMOUFLAGE METHODS - CONCEALING OBJECTS

Hiding is the concealment of an object by some form of physical screen. Hiding is accomplished by using thick vegetation or terrain features that screen vehicles from ground observation. In some cases, the screen itself can be invisible to detection and, at times, it is the overt screen that protects the activity or equipment from observation.

Blending is the arrangement or application of camouflage materials on, over, or around an object so that it appears to be part of the background. Blending distinctly man -made objects into a natural terrain pattern is necessary to maintain a normal and natural appearance.

Disguising involves the simulation of an object or activity so that it looks like something else.

CAMOUFLAGE CONSIDERATIONS

In preparing for covert remote area operations, position selection, reflection reduction, and concealment are conditions the Team must consider.

Position Selection

Siting or position selection is of critical importance in any environment but particularly so in arid areas. Site positions that fit into the existing ground pattern with minimum alteration to the terrain. The sites selected should suppress ground observation. Some areas such as valley floors might have sparse vegetation, but adjacent wadis could offer thicker vegetation with opportunities for defilade and enhanced potential for concealment from aerial threats. Day laagers should not be areas that would be obvious to locals.

Reflection Reduction

Reducing surfaces that reflect light is a measure that starts in base before deploying by removing mirrors and covering headlights and taillights. Normally the windshield is not removed so that it can provide protection from blowing sand, dust, and rocks thrown by the vehicle in front. Team members cover all reflective surfaces with a close weave, non-see-through cloth (canvas or target cloth). A sight portal must remain open for driving. If cloth or other material is not available, mix water and dirt to get mud and apply it to the reflective surfaces.

Concealment

Usually the most effective way to conceal vehicles is by the use of netting. Military camouflage nets are available from surplus stores. These nets provide concealment from visual, near IR, and radar and target acquisition devices. This net is not intended as a complete camouflage system as it depends on its imitation of the ground surface, both color and texture, to be effective. Alternatives to the military camouflage net are—

Open weave cloth with patchwork colored to match the terrain in the operational area. This type of net might be the preferred choice if operating in a predominantly sand dune area.

Large fishing net garnished with burlap to suit the color of the operational area.

Vegetation can be added to this net to enhance concealment.

NOTE: When using netting in open areas, drape the net over the vehicle and slope the sides gradually to the ground. Break up the outline of the vehicle by placing props or poles underneath and intertwine vegetation into the net. Eliminate shadows caused by the vehicle or net. In broken country, use the drape to tie the net to some irregularity in the terrain, such as next to a thick scrubby shrub or small tree. Break up the outline and eliminate shadows. After placing the net, cut and place vegetation into the net to add realism, texture, and similarity to the terrain and to help break up the outline.

CHAPTER 9

EXFILTRATION TECHNIQUES

There are two methods of exfiltration available when conducting covert rural/remote area surveillance - normal and emergency.

Normal Exfiltration. After the successful completion of the operation, activate the planned exfiltration plan. Little is gained if the detailed information gathered can't get out of the operational area in time to act on. Likewise, if you are compromised by the target or it discovers abandoned observation sites overlooking a complex, it will change the target's structure. Then when the arresting police arrive, they may find an alert or absconded target. This type of situation works in favor of the target and must be avoided at all cost. The following paragraphs outline the rules that must be followed when writing a normal exfiltration plan.

Ensure pick up points are far enough away from the target to mask the sounds and lights of the exfiltration vehicle. Use mountains, dense foliage, and other like terrain features to your advantage. Under normal conditions, in open, flat terrain, on a calm night, even helicopters and speed boats lose most of their audible signature at about 5 kilometers.

While exfiltrating, use obstacles to your advantage. Move so that ridge lines, rivers, and other like areas are between the target and the planned pickup points. Avoid areas with regularly trafficked roads or trails.

Plan for extra movement time in the exfiltration phase. If the maps used for movement planning were wrong, pickup time could be missed and jeopardize the operation mission. Plan to move off target the night before exfiltration. Such movement gives the extra time to pass around unforeseen danger areas. It also ensures you are in fact at the correct place for pickup on time.

Primary and alternate pickup points are never on a single compass bearing away from the target. If arriving at the first pickup point, but exfiltration is not effected, ensure the alternate pickup point is in a different direction to avoid trackers and possible team compromise contact.

Take care to avoid detection during the mission and after exfiltration. Take out everything brought into the area. Burn rubbish such as retort pouch meal wrappers using a firelighter or hexamine heat tab, which produces very little light or smoke with only the tin foil remaining. The tin foil, when compressed, can form a small ball, reducing the overall bulk greatly. Replace, compact, and camouflage soil from all digging. Before departing the positions, make a final check of the area. Check for even the smallest details.

Emergency Exfiltration. If detected or engaged by civilians or the target themselves, exfiltrate by preplanned emergency means. This exfiltration requires either activation of an Evasion plan or the deployment of armed police teams to come to the rescue.

Exfiltration of Information. When time-critical information needs to be passed to the tasking authority, you can pass the information in several ways. You can send short messages to the supporting base station by many means. Burst transmissions are the best method for countering target or media monitoring efforts. Masking the radio sites behind hills or mountains prevents some of the same problems.

RURAL COMMUNICATIONS

Radio communications used by surveillance operators are very dependent on line of sight and distance (mainly UHF) for reliable clear communications. A thorough appreciation of the terrain will dictate whether UHF is practicable or whether you need to consider HF or satcom communications. You might decide to use a combination of UHF (area of operation) and HF (contact with operations command) to achieve the best communications network.

The nature of the terrain will also strongly influence where it is best to set up an observation post, so as to guarantee communications.

Another example of communications effected by terrain is where a large hill is between you and your receiving station, effecting clear and reliable communications. Standard hand held UHF surveillance radios, operating without the aid of a repeater station, will be blocked by the hill as their effective range in these conditions is very limited.

If you are observing on foot, the problem is solved simply by moving location. If you are in an observation post that provides great visual coverage and security, it may not be prudent for you to move purely because of poor communications.

The better solution might be to set up a portable repeater station (this would be arranged through the technical support group) or a manned relay station. There might be times where you will be in an isolated location where terrain and vegetation don't allow any other form of communication other than HF or satcom. This type of communications is unaffected by terrain and vegetation because it does not rely on line of sight. HF bounces radio waves off the ionosphere (outer regions of the earth's atmosphere) and then back to earth. This method of communications is very effective over long distances (eg: thousands of kilometres). Similarly, satcom communications are not effected by terrain or vegetation because it bounces the radio waves off a satellite orbiting the earth.

<u>APPENDIX A: SAMPLE RURAL SURVEILLANCE EQUIPMENT LIST:</u>

3-day operation in Temperate Region on foot

BASIC LIST:

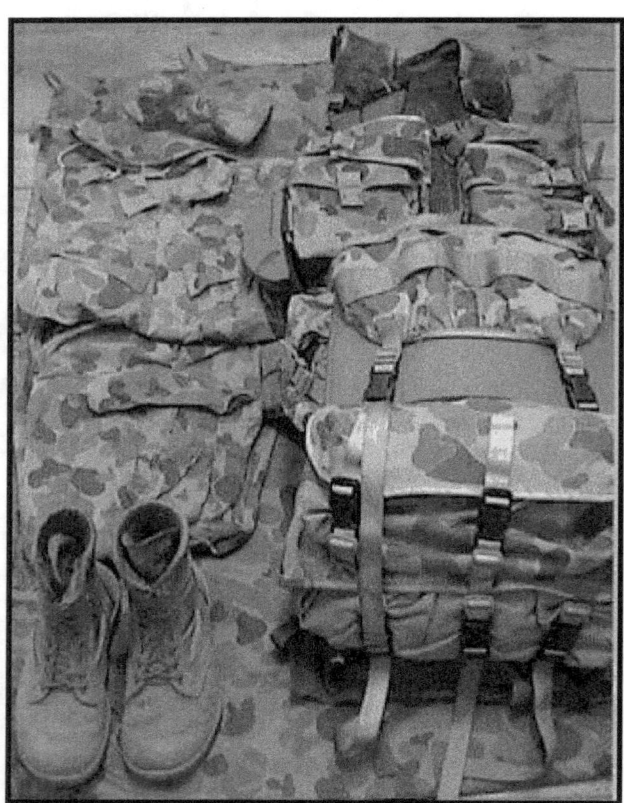

Clothing:

Camouflage Shirt
Camouflage Trousers
Camouflage bush hat
Combat-type boots Green
nomex gloves

Load-Bearing Equipment:

Camera Vest (camouflage painted) Army
belt

2 x Army water bottle pouches

2 x Army ammunition pouches
Backpack (camouflage painted)

Shelter & Sleeping Gear:

Green or camouflage groundsheet

Lightweight sleeping bag

Sleeping pad

Rain jacket (earth colour)

Wool or fleece jumper

Balaclava (acrylic or Thinsulate)

Water/Cooking/Food:

2 x water bottles

2 litre Camelbak water bag
Plastic Spoon

Pocket Knife

Army Canteen Cup

Canteen Cup stove

2 x boxes Hexamine fuel

3 days food (eaten cold if necessary)

Cigarette Lighter

Personal:

Camouflage paint

Wine Bladder (urinal)

Heavy-duty ziplock bags (toilet/rubbish)

Small packet wet ones

Personal First Aid Kit

Communications:

UHF radio

Throat mic/earpiece unit

6 x spare batteries for radio

Navigation/illumination:

Map of Target Area

Air photo mosaic of Target Area

Compass

GPS receiver

Mini Maglite with red lens

4 x spare batteries for mini Maglite

Observation/recording:

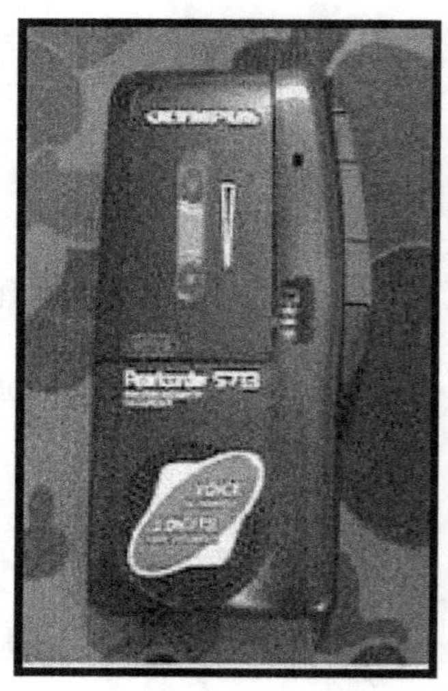

DV video camera

Mini Tripod

4 x spare tapes

3 x spare camera batteries

Mini spotting scope

2 x Notebooks

2 x Pencils

2 x Micro cassette recorder

4 x micro cassette tapes

4 x sets spare batteries for micro cassette recorder

OP construction:

Folding shovel

Secateurs/light bolt cutters

Camouflage net

Hessian

Hootchie cord

Shock corded fibreglass tent poles

Camouflage painted chicken wire strips

www.ingramcontent.com/pod-product-compliance
Lightning Source LLC
Chambersburg PA
CBHW081317250726
48662CB00008B/2623